RETAIL ARBITRAGE

How To Arbitrage Successfully Online

By Erik Smith

Table Of Contents

Introduction 1
Understanding the Opportunity 2
Understanding the Pros and Cons...4
Getting Started...9
Choosing Your Products...12
Tips for Success...17
Conclusion 19

Free Stuff

Do you want to get notified when I have free books? Then sign up for my newsletter. I will never spam you. I will only send you valuable stuff that you can use to help you improve your life.

Sign up here - http://forms.aweber.com/form/26/1968511626.htm

Disclaimer

This document is geared towards providing exact and reliable information in regards to the topic and issue covered. The publication is sold with the idea that the publisher is not required to render accounting, officially permitted, or otherwise, qualified services. If advice is necessary, legal or professional, a practiced individual in the profession should be ordered.

- From a Declaration of Principles which was accepted and approved equally by a Committee of the American Bar Association and a Committee of Publishers and Associations.

In no way is it legal to reproduce, duplicate, or transmit any part of this document in either electronic means or in printed format. Recording of this publication is strictly prohibited and any storage of this document is not allowed unless with written permission from the publisher. All rights reserved.

The information provided herein is stated to be truthful and consistent, in that any liability, in terms of inattention or otherwise, by any usage or abuse of any policies, processes, or directions contained within is the solitary and utter responsibility of the recipient reader. Under no circumstances will any legal responsibility or blame be held against the publisher for any reparation, damages, or monetary loss due to the information herein, either directly or indirectly.

Respective authors own all copyrights not held by the publisher.

The information herein is offered for informational purposes solely, and is universal as so. The presentation of the information is without contract or any type of guarantee assurance.

The trademarks that are used are without any consent, and the publication of the trademark is without permission or backing by the trademark owner. All trademarks and brands within this book are for clarifying purposes only and are the owned by the owners themselves, not affiliated with this document.

INTRODUCTION

Retail arbitrage is a simple business model. First, a retailer sells a product for a certain price. Second, you purchase that product and resell it for a higher price. Third, you keep the profit. It doesn't matter if that product is being sold online or in-store. What matters is that the price it's being sold for allows you to make a profit through reselling.

But even if retail arbitrage looks like a simple process of reselling products, it's not all about that. While the method may be similar, there's more to consider if you are doing retail arbitrage. One of those things is understanding the opportunity that brings about re-sellable products. Another thing is understanding the benefits and threats that retail arbitrage poses.

Yet another thing to consider is how to get started. You simply can't walk in to Wal-Mart, for example, pick the products you want to sell, buy them in bulk, and then go off to resell them. There's more to simply finding and choosing the right product for you.

On top of getting started is how you can keep things going. Realize that when you start on something like retail arbitrage, it's not too simple to quit. That's especially if you are having fun doing it, while enjoying the profit it brings.

Still, staying in the business of retail arbitrage is one thing. Being successful in it is another. There are people out there who are sharing that they quit their full time job because they're doing great in retail arbitrage. What are their secrets? This mini ebook answers all these questions.

Throughout its discussion, it will involve online marketplaces like Amazon, Alibaba, eBay, and Facebook Markets, as well as physical stores like Wal-Mart, Target, and other leading retail companies.

At the end of this book, readers should have a clear understanding of the basic principles involving retail arbitrage, how they can get started on it, how they may grow from it, and how they may succeed in it.

UNDERSTANDING THE OPPORTUNITY

Why would someone be interested in buying products to resell from a retailer instead of a supplier? That's a valid question. The thing is, in retail arbitrage, you don't simply buy a product for its price. The secret lies in finding retail products that are on sale, that are discounted – however you name it as long as the original retail price has been cut.

Why would a retailer put products on sale in the first place? Have you ever wondered about that? Well, the primary reason is clearance. Retailers have a definite quantity of products per category and per brand per day.

For example, a retailer is consistent about having only 200 bar soaps of brand X on its shelves per day, so it must sell those 200 soaps because another 200 of it are going to be delivered the next day.

If only 100 of those soaps will sell in a given day, the store will expect a total of 300 soaps it needs to sell the next day. And the numbers keep piling up each day that the store fails to dispose of the soap. What happens after that?

The store may be able to accommodate the daily delivery of soaps by placing the excess quantities in its warehouse. The thing is, a warehouse is limited by its physical area. Because a store cannot exclusively sell a bar soap in all its shelves, it has to make room for other products.

So if the same is the case for the retailer's other products, then the warehouse would end up getting chaotic with unsold products. That's when retailers, with the drive to clear their shelves, offer selected products at a discount.

As a consumer, you may notice that at times, your favorite retailer seems to be giving away a product at a dirt-cheap price when it was selling it for a higher price before. This tells you that your retailer may be intent on disposing the product for good.

Why does this happen in the first place?

The answer lies on consumer behavior. And that behavior heavily influences the law of supply and demand. To illustrate, that soap the retailer is selling may be popular among its customers for six months and counting. In fact, it may have been a best-seller. This drives up demand.

In response, the retailer seeks to fulfill that demand by asking for more supplies. So it arranges an order from the supplier for X amount of soap to be delivered daily. In our example, that's 200 soaps.

However, there comes a time when the bar soap will just be another selection on the shelf. It could be that another variant of the soap has come out, it could be that a competitor has a better soap to offer – anything could have happened leading to declining sales.

So while demand is falling, the supplies keep coming. The result? More soaps; less buyers. This scenario is when retailers introduce strategies in order to make sure that the soap sells. One of those strategies is by giving the soap's price a hefty discount.

But why can't these retailers simply return excess stock? They can do that, but they may not have the time or the manpower to oversee the return process. See, these retailers operate in a way that products have to move from their shelves in a quick manner. They simply don't have the time to market a certain product that's currently underselling. They have to sell stuff as quickly as they can.

So the opportunity has presented itself when people thought about making money out of these heavily discounted goods. And with the rise of online marketplaces like Amazon and Alibaba, some people have further realized that they can acquire products online and resell them online just the same.

So what these people have done all these years is now collectively represented by a business model called 'retail arbitrage.' It is a business model that can be executed offline or online. But is this business model the ultimate model? Let's take a look at the pros and cons in the next chapter.

UNDERSTANDING THE PROS AND CONS

Retail arbitrage can be done in two ways

You have the option of doing two things under this business model. First, you can source for discounted products online and purchase them. And then you can choose to resell the same products online or on a physical storefront.

Second, you can source for discounted products by visiting your favorite retailers and looking at what's on sale. And then you can resell their products online or in a physical location. Of course the third one is a combination of both. Regardless, you can source and resell online or offline.

Retail arbitrage doesn't require a physical storefront

Before the introduction of websites, social media business pages, and online marketplaces, people had to find a way to display their products before customers. Selling in flea markets is one of the still profitable strategies today.

But with the dawn of digital promotion and marketing, people are now considering selling their products online more than actually going to a physical place to sell. Now, they do not feel pressured about putting up physical storefronts because they can showcase their products online.

Retail arbitrage doesn't require resellers to have their own digital storefronts

Not having to worry about putting up a storefront is beneficial enough for resellers. But not having to worry about a digital storefront is even better. That's because not all resellers are familiar with e-commerce websites, let alone can afford investing in website development.

Now, resellers can sell on Facebook, on Amazon, on Craigslist, on eBay, on Alibaba, etc. Online marketplaces offer a digital storefront for resellers even if this only means a listing space for their products and not a functional landing page or a fully designed e-commerce website.

Real arbitrage doesn't require a hefty amount of capital

Believe it or not, depending on the product, and whether or not you resell on an online platform, your $200 can get you a long way. It can net you a profit relative to the margin that you set and the resell price that you offer.

And because a measly 'startup capital' is needed, resellers don't have to worry about overhead costs as well. The idea of having to pay employees, rent, utility bills, and specialty personnel like accountants requires a significant amount of investment money.

Retail arbitrage can be your gateway to private labeling

Private labeling is yet another business model that closely resembles retail arbitrage. That's both business models involve reselling a product. However, with private label, you are reselling someone else's product with an icing on top: you get to display your branding on the product.

With the original product brand taken out of the equation, you now have the advantage of creating your brand identity. If that's established enough, you can take advantage of the publicity in order to add more product lines to your offering.

Retail arbitrage is simple to execute

You can be successful as a reseller under this model provided that you are cautious about what you're doing. Always remember that anyone can find success in any business model as long as due diligence and the right mix of mindset, research, and even mentorship comes into play.

Because retail arbitrage is a simple business model, you may get a little sloppy. So stick to the basics: not all products you resell will actually sell, you may not have a free reign over the products you are reselling, and you make mistakes unexpectedly along the way.

As simple and encouraging retail arbitrage is, especially for starting entrepreneurs, there are flipsides that you need to keep in mind as well.

Brand gating for some products is possible

When a product is brand gated, you need to ask the brand for permission to resell their products. So that cookery set that you're eyeing to resell for a cheaper price may not be within reach because the brand that carries it prefers to sell it to an affluent market.

On top of brands brand gating their product agreement with their distributors or direct resellers, it is also possible that the same agreement is signed with online marketplaces. This means that if a brand has signed a brand gating agreement with Amazon, for example, there is no way that you can sell their products on the platform. You would have to look elsewhere.

You don't own any of the products that you sell

This means you don't really have control over the things you sell. It may not look problematic at first glance but this may cause a headache on your end once you realize that the demand for the thing you sell is higher than what you have in your inventory.

Your natural response would be to order more items of that product in order to replenish your inventory. The thing is, sometimes, original retailers impose buying limits. This is your purchase ceiling. You go over the ceiling, you can't purchase any more items.

So you think that that's OK because the retailer you're working with has branches in other areas. So you drive to the other branches just to place an order for your product line. And until your stock is replenished, you will continue to check other branches for their items.

What you don't realize is that the process of doing so has already cost you an overhead for fuel and mileage for your car. More than that, you already have lost time and have spent much energy to get what you want. All because of the buying limit.

So buying limits can take a toll on your price point. And it's rather difficult for you as a reseller to increase your price point, especially when your customers already know the price ranges that you offer.

Your profit depends on your inventory

Unless you ask and unless they tell you, retailers don't go about revealing why certain products are on sale, etc. That's especially true if you are a reseller. This is to say that you should have a working knowledge on the products that are given a hefty discount.

But do you know when your retailer will actually put a product on sale? Will they even tell you why they're doing it? And what products will be given the next discount? Will they tell you just so you can get ready? A safe bet would be no.

So this is real: your profit is totally dependent on what you have on stock. That's because people will either love it, like it, or ignore it. You can do a little promotion of some sort but the buying decision always lies on your customers.

One thing you should be careful of is buying products in physical retail stores without doing a little homework. It can be that they're putting products on sale because a newer version is on its way. It can also be that they're on sale because of a product defect or a recall. A retailer going on sale because they've overstocked or they're doing clearance is nice. But for other reasons? You should do your homework.

Amazon's Brand Registry Protection may be a threat

If you're using Amazon for retail arbitrage, you need to carefully read what its Brand Registry Protection is about. Of a particular interest to you would be how the BRP is helping protect its listed brands. With all the infringement going around, it's but right to protect the rightful owners of patents, etc.

However, there is also a downside. Since the BRP gives brands and private labels more control of their products, retail arbitrage resellers may be tagged as unauthorized resellers. Worse, they can be flagged as people who sell counterfeit products. How so?

There's a great chance that retail arbitrage resellers provide one benefit to their customers: a lower price point. For a brand or a private label that does not want to go below a specific price point, they have every right to be concerned when faced with someone who does.

Then again, everyone has a reason for setting a price point like that. You may have gotten your product for a ridiculously very low price so you can sell it for a price low enough to still net you a profit. But that's not how it works for some brands and private labels. It's something you should be on the lookout for.

At this point, you've been given the essential information that you need about retail arbitrage. If you decide to give it a try, then turn to the next chapter to find out how get started.

GETTING STARTED

Step 1. Have your bank account ready

You will never know when you're going to make your first sale. Besides, if you hook up with Amazon, then they'll need your bank information to process credits to your account. You can take in payment through PayPal as well, but then, the funds will have to go to your bank account at a certain point just the same.

When you have a bank account ready, make sure that it is opened for the purpose of keeping your business money. That's because a sound advice has been resonating all throughout: take your earnings and invest it back to your business. You can't have your business profits cover for your personal expenditures. Let your business money roll where it should be rolling: your business.

Step 2. Choose a platform

Unless you decide to keep your reselling operations offline through a physical store, you need a place where you can resell online. Two of the most popular online marketplaces for retail arbitragers are Amazon and eBay. Each has its own advantages and disadvantages.

For Amazon, its A-Z campaign has been proven questionable. That's because despite it selling a variety of products in different categories, there are items that some people just can't find. However, it is undeniable that most people who shop online shop on Amazon.

But if you're interested in reselling rare or novelty items, choose eBay. Across the years, eBay has created its own market. People who are looking for strange, creepy, weird, vintage, or hard-to-find items flock to the platform.

You can also do business on both platforms as long as you know where your target audience is for the product that you intend to resell.

Now, you can totally pass up on these platforms, but there's a huge advantage to them - especially on Amazon.

For one, Amazon's FBA program (Fulfilled by Amazon), only requires you to send the physical product to their warehouse and they'll take care of the rest. That's from listing to shipping your product when someone orders from the platform.

Two, you may be able to sell more quickly because your product will be under the Amazon brand. Your product won't have an Amazon printed or engraved on it, but it will be displayed under the Amazon flagship.

Step 3. Invest in the right tools

Almost everyone has a smartphone. If you don't have one, you have to get one because it will help you a great deal. With the internet functionality that smartphones have, you can now download the application of your chosen platform, as well as other apps that can help you in your reselling business.

However, if you decide to pass up any of the online marketplace platforms, there's a good chance that you need to have the following in order to get your product out to an online audience:

- An e-commerce website that has a payment processing functionality

- A social media business page where you can promote your products

In other words, you need a place online in order to sell.

Also familiarize yourself with tools like ScanPower. This is a tool used by retail arbitragers who are using Amazon's FBA. You may also need a scanner that is synched to your phone. Depending on how you want to take on retail arbitraging, you should arm yourself with the right tools to help you achieve your goals.

Step 4. Go out there

You know by now that you can find low-priced products anywhere online that you can purchase and resell. However, don't forget that money also lies in thrift shops, flea markets, garage sales, local retailers, and the huge retailers that you know today.

It's all about being hands-on so that you'll learn the different facets of retail arbitraging. If you find that you have more luck trying to find products online that actually sell, then settle with it. But if you know that there can be gems out there as well, then go for it. You can't really tell what your next best-seller will be.

Step 5. Continue learning

In almost everything, learning happens on-the-job. This is applicable to retail arbitraging as well. But what you shouldn't ignore doing is learning from the people who have done it and who have succeeded in it. Online, there are lots of resources focusing on retail arbitrage. Some of these resources were written by people who have found success in the business model.

Be hungry for knowledge. Learn about how people achieved success, learn about where and how they failed, and learn about what they've done in response to the challenges that they've encountered. Most of all, learn about their values and how they put these values into practice in order to achieve success.

In the next chapter, you'll find answers to some of the most difficult questions beginner retail arbitragers ask.

CHOOSING YOUR PRODUCTS

What makes a good product to resell? There is a few criteria that defines an ideal product for reselling under retail arbitrage. Take a look at them below.

PROFIT MARGIN

Products that have a 40% or more profit margin, by rule of thumb, are good products for retail arbitrage. A profit margin is an amount indicating that your revenue from selling a product is exceeding the cost in your business. The profit margin can be calculated as follows:

(Gross Profit / Revenue) x 100 = Profit Margin

Where,

Revenue – Cost = Gross Profit

To illustrate, a profit margin of 25% is derived as follows:

$200 - $150 = $50

50 / 200 = 0.25 x 100 = 25%

Why the profit margin of 40%. That's because it allows you to turn in a profit despite competition from more reputable brands selling the same product for the same price. Should that happen, you can easily undercut your price without sacrificing your profit.

It also allows you to unload your inventory in the event that a competitor is offering a substantial discount. Say, your competitor is offering the same product for a 20% discount, you can lower your price point and may still manage to move your inventory because you are operating well within the 40% profit margin.

But then again remember that the 40% profit margin is just an arbitrary number. You can still end up losing money in the process, but that's how the game is played. The percentage is only a recommendation for beginners. Once you get a hand on retail arbitraging, you can definitely set your profit margin.

PRICE POINT

Settle with products that are neither cheap nor too expensive. A common tip from retail arbitragers is to settle for products that are within the $10 and $30 range. Going lower than $10 may yield a smaller profit margin and going higher than $30 may mean that you're investing too much on a single product.

If you buy a $10 product, you may have at least a $4 profit margin. This is in accordance to the 40% rule. While that may seem small, it may multiply based on the quantity of items that you sell for that product. But why $10 and not $5 to be safe?

Remember that there are competitors out there who may offer the same product you have for a price lower than $10. If you compete with them and end up undercutting your price point, your profit margin may effectively diminish, yielding you nothing. So that's a loss on your end.

In addition, remember that you will have to ship the products on your own or, if you're working with Amazon's FBA, you have to pay them a cut for every item that ships from their warehouse. The shipping cost can be quite a burden to you if you're doing this alone, but not so much if you do it with Amazon. They give discounts on shipping items subject to terms and conditions. Still, shipping money is a cost to your business. So if you're pricing your item $5 or below, then your profit will be affected.

Likewise, if you price your products above $30, you may be in for a higher risk. That's because people are wise enough to check on potentially lower prices for the same product on the market. While the purchase decision ultimately lies on the buyer, there's always room for hesitation if they see that the same product has a lower price on the other side. The result: your inventory will not move.

Then again, remember that the higher you go, the higher margin you can make. This translates to higher income. One advantage of offering a higher price point is that your competition is cut down. A lot of sellers offer cheap products and not a lot of them are willing to go higher. Still, you should exercise caution when reselling a product at a higher price.

PRODUCT DIMENSIONS

If you notice, most items on sale online are those that are light and small. But some, especially specialty brands, can sell heavy items as well. How is this relevant?

The product dimensions become relevant only in the context of shipping. You're well aware that packages are being weighed at which the weight becomes the basis of your shipping charge. If you're reselling on your own, you may get hit with shipping costs. However, resellers on FBA report that Amazon offers them low rates on UPS.

When you're operating on your own, you also need to factor in the product dimension in terms of your comfort. Would it be ok with you to carry bulky packages on your way to shipping them? Would it be ok with you to personally package items that are bulky? Think about convenience.

PRODUCT REVIEW

Note that we're talking about retail products here so there's a good chance that if you're doing retail arbitrage online, the product you want has a review. That review can be in Amazon, eBay or another online marketplace. So if a product has predominantly bad reviews, would you still consider reselling it?

Another dilemma for you is when confronted with a product that equally has positive and negative reviews. At this point, it will be your decision as a reseller on whether to take your chances. Besides, no product out there has been solely given positive reviews by consumers.

One of the things that you can do is to look at top reviews. These are reviews that are popular and are recommended by other users who feel the same way about the product. From there, you can weigh in on your options.

If you feel compelled to buy a product despite it having bad reviews, then stop. You're just letting your emotions cloud over your better judgment.

One rule of thumb you should remember is to buy products that actually sell; not products you like.

IN-DEMAND PRODUCTS

A good example to benchmark your selection process is to look at Amazon's bestseller list. This list contains items that are selling faster with more quantities than the rest. While checking, always keep in mind to not fall for the concepts of scarcity and timeliness.

If you feel compelled to purchase a product because you think that tomorrow may no longer be a good time, think twice about it. Today's top picks may only be prompted by a fad. Tomorrow, they'd drop off the list. If you ignore this fact, you may end up buying something that goes out-of-date tomorrow.

So when you look at products that are in-demand, assess their longevity. Will they still be a bestseller even after, say, 10 days? Make your decision based on the homework that you've done.

PRODUCTS WITH FEW SELLERS

If there are few sellers for a product, then it may be a good time for you to enter their niche and compete with them. And when we say 'competition,' we mean not just the price point but also your reputation as a reseller. While fewer sellers mean lesser competition, it's worth checking what the product they're selling is.

Ask yourself: is the product a fast-seller? Does the product price fall within your target profit margin? What about the logistics? Will you be bothered by packaging the product and them by shipping costs?

Eventually, if a product is a fast-seller, it will attract the attention of other sellers who think exactly like you. Just as we discussed under the prior point, it pays to think logically before making a decision.

So apart from Amazon, eBay and other known online marketplaces, where can you source potential products for reselling? Check the following:

Deal sites. These websites offer an array of discounted or limited-quantity products that you can score with significant price cuts. Some examples are fatwallet.com, dealsplus.com, become.com, techbargains.com, dealnews.com, and pricegrabber.com. Just search for 'deal sites' and you'll get tons of results.

Big retailers. Yes, it will involve the physical effort of getting somewhere but that 30% discount on selected products at Wal-Mart or Macy's? That's hard to ignore because it can offer you relevant profit margins if you know how to price your buys.

Thrift shops and retail shops. You will have to scour the store to find sellable products. But as we mentioned, there's money on the table for great finds.

Flea markets. There's a reason people flock to flea markets: to take advantage of cheap products that would have been expensive if they buy it somewhere else. And although finding a potential item to resell on flea market is more of a stroke of luck, you'll get lucky if you discover a treasure trove.

Garage sales. Yes, there are potentially re-sellable items to be found in garage sales. And while these items are more of products that are used, you can upcycle them (if you have the skill) in order to command a higher price point.

So while you're at it, what should you be doing in order to stay on track and to achieve success? Find out in the final chapter.

TIPS FOR SUCCESS

BECOME A SPECIALIST

Choose a niche category where you want to specialize in. For example, if you want to resell men's accessories, you can resell neck and bow ties, cuff links, scarves, bracelets, wallets, and so on. When you pick your niche, stick to it. Take care of it because you may become known as the go-to reseller for these items.

ENSURE GOOD ITEM CONDITION

Even if a product is used, you have to make sure that it is functional and that it has minimal defects. If you're keen on reselling a product with minimal defects, say so in your product description. A great way to build transparency is to take a photo of the defect. This way, people can see it. Some people can accept minimal product defects, so it pays to let them know beforehand.

KNOW WHERE AND WHEN TO SOURCE

Some retailers are known to execute a flash sale but some of them are pretty predictable when it comes to doing clearance or discounted sales. Know when your target store usually does its sales so that you'll be ready to pounce. Also, despite not announcing it, some stores have a dedicated aisle for items on clearance or at a discount. Know where to find those.

ASK EMPLOYEES

At times, retailers are itching to clear some of their inventory. However, they don't know how to do that the fastest way because there's really no room in-store to display everything for clearance. Often, employees know about this but they don't proactively offer them to buyers. The good news is, you can ask. And if there's one, you may end up finding not just a small room of jackpot items but an entire container of it.

SOURCE WITH AN OPEN MIND

Just because you consider an item to be junk doesn't mean that no one will pay good money for it. If you source your products, keep in mind that your target market needs more than what you're offering them. What you think merely as a $10 object may mean $100 to someone who ends up purchasing it. It's all about what people need and it's all about the value that they place on a product.

BE ALERT AT CHECKOUT

Sometimes, the price tags on items may not be updated even if they are on sale. So while you're checking out, make sure that the item scan is consistent with the displayed discount price. You absolutely wouldn't want to pay more for any item because that will fall on your price point and on your profit margin.

ADAPT A BUSINESS MINDSET

You're doing something business-like after all. So in everything you do, you should act like a business owner. Protect your interests while upholding those of your customers'. It can take a while to build a group of advocates because you have to earn people's trust. Once trust is in place, you'll be able to prompt a word-of-mouth kind of recommendations from your clients.

So as you continue to resell, practice consistency and transparency. Always do everything in good faith. When you reach a certain level of consistency, your customers will readily know what to expect from you.

Also don't forget that a business-minded person knows better than to mix his or her personal life with his business life. This includes bank accounts. As much as possible, you should have a business account where you can manage your money from your sales. You're operating a business, and if you have what it takes, your business may grow and will open a whole new set of possibilities.

CONCLUSION

No business model is an absolute model for everyone. More often, finding the right recipe with respect to the nature of a business involves trials and errors, making mistakes, and yes, failing. What retail arbitraging does is that it offers an option for people to hone their entrepreneurial spirit. It is one among the many types of business opportunities that are out there.

Because it doesn't involve a huge financial commitment, it is an ideal path for beginner business people to take. However, as simple as it looks, there are still risks involved. That's why it pays to learn everything about retail arbitrage first before jumping into it.

This mini eBook has presented the typical scenario that led to retail arbitraging. It also presented some pros and cons, the steps to get started, and information about product sourcing and selection. Through these essential information, the author hopes that you'll have what you need to plan your way towards making retail arbitrage your ultimate business model.

Thank you for reading this book.

Free Stuff

Do you want to get notified when I have free books? Then sign up for my newsletter. I will never spam you. I will only send you valuable stuff that you can use to help you improve your life.

Sign up here - http://forms.aweber.com/form/26/1968511626.htm

www.ingramcontent.com/pod-product-compliance
Lightning Source LLC
Chambersburg PA
CBHW031941170526
45157CB00008B/3268